TABLE OF

Unless otherwise indicated, all Scripture quotations are taken from the King James Version of the Bible.
Twenty Keys To A Happier Marriage
Wisdom Key Books · ISBN 1-56394-036-1/B-55
Copyright © 1994 by **MIKE MURDOCK**
All publishing rights belong exclusively to Wisdom International
Publisher/Editor: Deborah Murdock Johnson
Published by The Wisdom Center · P. O. Box 99 · Denton, Texas 76202
1-888-WISDOM-1 (1-888-947-3661) · **Website: thewisdomcenter.tv**

1

RECOGNIZE THE IMPORTANCE GOD PLACES ON YOUR MARRIAGE.

Marriage Is Not An Experiment.
Marriage is a God-idea.
1. **Marriage Is The Divine Design For The Celebration Of Love.** It is the Divine Plan for the reproduction of the human race. It was not a human idea evolving from the imagination of a lonely man, Adam. It is the earthly picture of the spiritual union between the Church and Jesus.

God planned marriage.

God wants you to place great value on your marriage.

2. **Marriage Was More Than Moral Protection From The Temptation Of Immorality.** Other women did not yet exist.

Marriage was more than a shield from potential enemies. No enemy had yet appeared. Before satan ever revealed himself, emerged, God said, "...It is not good that man should be alone;" (Genesis 2:18).

3. **Marriage Was Not A Substitution For**

Work, Career Or A Productive Life. It was intended to be the Miracle of Completion, resolving the emotional emptiness in man.

Celebrate your marriage.

Protect your marriage.

Make your marriage the Priority Focus of your life.

DISCERN THAT SATAN IS THE ENEMY TO YOUR MARRIAGE.

Your Home Has An Enemy.
Anything Good Is Despised By Everything Evil. So, you have an invisible adversary.

1. Every Gift From God Will Be Contested By Satan. The Holy Spirit recorded a fascinating conversation between God and satan... regarding the blessings of Job. Satan was wroth and infuriated that the pleasure and prosperity of Job had become one of the great pleasures and delights of God, His Provider.

What pleasures you incenses satan.

2. Satan Wants To Place Thorns In Your Nest...Marriage. He continually observes the plans of God. Anything receiving the attention of God instantly receives the attention of hell.

3. Satan Wants To Be The Third Party In Your Marriage Partnership. He wants to agitate...anger...disappoint. Using your weaknesses, he inspires unrealistic expectations, diverts your focus from servanthood to self-absorption. He fuels your imagination through television and relationships...until the presence of God is splintered and ceases to be the goal of your union.

4. Continuously Scan Your Environment For An Adversarial Entry. Look for any symptom of satanic strategy.

Fight to keep keenly aware of satanic inroads. *Become the Watchman over your home.*

RECOMMENDED BOOKS:
B-07   Battle Techniques For War Weary Saints (32 pages/$3)

 3

ANTICIPATE AND RESIST ANY INFLUENCE INJECTING ANGER, FEAR OR STRIFE INTO YOUR HOME CLIMATE.

Thoughts Have Presence.

You can walk into a home and sense confusion, bitterness, doubt, jealousy or joy. The attitude, energy, enthusiasm or sorrow of the human spirit is contagious.

One lady shared an interesting discovery with me. When a close friend went on her vacation, her relationship with her husband instantly improved. In fact, it seemed strife-free...until her friend returned. Then, the contention and friction reappeared. Reluctantly but firmly, she accepted that evil communications corrupt good manners. Each friendship is an ingredient that changes the equation of your life.

One husband noted that certain television shows nurtured an unsettling sexual restlessness within him. He was comparing his wife with the sensuality of the performers.

A young wife identified the timing of unexplainable jealousy toward her husband...after watching her favorite soap opera on television.

Every emotion has a birthplace, a beginning.

Stay watchful, vigilant and sensitive to any changes in the environment of your home or inner life.

Never Complain About
What You Permit.

-MIKE MURDOCK

The Role Of Every Parent
Is To Decide
Who Influences Their Child.

-MIKE MURDOCK

DECIDE THE HEROES, KNOWLEDGE AND INFLUENCES YOUR FAMILY NEEDS.

Your Home Is Your Palace.

1.   Decide The Climate That Dominates Your House. Remember these factors: words permitted, disorder allowed, colors of the walls, television programs, choice of music, scented candles.

2.   Carefully Design A Specific Strategy That Creates That Environment. My mother was a master at it. She sculptured the music we heard...the instruments of piano, accordion, guitar. She carefully selected the biographies of Uncommon Achievers who would become our childhood heroes.

3.   Invest Significant Time In Visualizing The Perfect Atmosphere. What is The Dream Environment...that you want to be in your home? Find pictures in magazines or books that clarify this inner photograph.

4.   Create Your Library List Of Heroes. Collect books on them. Discuss those whose greatness affected millions.   Who are the Top Ten

Champions of Greatness that you are teaching your children to admire?

5. Choose Four Marriage Conferences To Attend Annually. This *Preventive* Planning ...accesses Mentorship that will prevent the decay of your relationship...every 90 days.

Some walls reveal our past.

6. Use The Walls Of Your Home To Announce The Future You Are Pursuing.

What You See Determines What You Desire.

What You Keep Seeing You Begin To Believe.

Carefully Choose A Home Church That Reflects Your Beliefs.

Your Church Reveals Your Priorities.

Some churches are chosen because they are conveniently close. Some churches are chosen because they are publicized and well-known.

1. Recognize The Pastor Whose Counsel Is From The Heart Of The Holy Spirit. You should choose a pastor who is a true spiritual Mentor, unleashing a new passion for The Word of God.

2. Make Your Church The Center Of Your Activities, Interest And Time. Limit career participation...school games...or whatever. But, always, make your Spiritual Life the first Priority of your time and attention.

3. Create A List Of Your Personal Spiritual Concerns. This includes the basic foundation truths that you view important and vital.

**4. Discern What Involvement And Time The Holy Spirit Wants You To Invest Into

Your Church Family And Goals. You may want to teach, sing in the choir or host a monthly Scriptural Success Breakfast for the business persons in your church.

Your church should be your Mentorship Center. Never trivialize this decision that decides the quality of your life.

6

ASK QUESTIONS THAT REVEAL YOUR RESPECT FOR THE OPINIONS OF YOUR PARTNER.

Marriage Is Access.

The opinions, observations and discoveries of others can unlock a new level of understanding. Invest time to listen, learn and evaluate the suggestions, needs and desires of your mate and children.

1. Your Mate Is Your Personal Confidante. You chose them to be your best friend. Their counsel is critical.

2. Your Passion To Pleasure Is Contagious. When you master the Art of Pleasure... toward your partner...you will unleash an indescribable influence on your environment.

3. Your Questions Reveal Your Caring. Create a personal list of questions you want answered about the pain, memories, dreams, fears of your mate...Your Best Friend.

4. Your Willingness To Listen Becomes A Portrait Of Your Humility. Listen long enough for the hidden emotions to be expressed. Listen carefully enough to collect sufficient under-standing. Listen accurately...so you can assess the true needs of your mate...that nobody else has been able to meet.

5. The Questions You Ask Decide The Answers You Discover.

You Have No Right To Anything You Have Not Pursued.

FOCUS ON THE FAVORABLE QUALITIES OF YOUR MATE THAT DISTINGUISH THEM FROM OTHERS.

Your Mate Is Unlike Anyone Else.

That's why you married! Some quality was the magnet that attracted you. Additional great qualities developed into a current that swiftly moved you into intimacy, confidentiality, commitment...and the Divine Covenant of Marriage.

1. Remember Your Chosen Focus Is The World You Have Decided To Create For Yourself. Your Focus Will Decide Your Feelings. When you focus on the admirable differences of your mate, you will instantly generate hope, warmth and cheerfulness.

2. List Seven Favorable Qualities Of Your Mate. Document them in your Private Journal. Do not trivialize any of them. If you can list more, do so. If these qualities were missing, your life would certainly become painful...in a day.

3. Verbalize Your Recognition Of Those

Qualities To Your Mate And Others. This births a climate of acceptance and caring where the Seeds of Love and Loyalty can grow.

4. **Expect The Divine Law Of Sowing And Reaping To Work In Your Favor.** Your Seeds of Love will grow.

Your Focus Always Decides Your Feelings.

Loyalty
Is The Proof
Of Character.

-MIKE MURDOCK

The Purpose
Of Forgiveness
Is Change.

-MIKE MURDOCK

USE THE IRRITATING TRAITS OF YOUR MATE AS MOTIVATION TO LEARN.

Pain Talks.

View every moment of irritation, pain and stress as a School of Discovery. Words are pictures of information. Conversations impart knowledge. Every human hurts. Somewhere. Some strive to escape their inner pain through their work...alcohol...illicit sex...drugs or even anger. So when the behavior of your mate agitates or even infuriates you, it is Learning Time. Time to listen and learn.

1. Learn About The Expectations Of Your Mate. Are they unrealistic? Were they unexpressed or unknown until this confrontation? Anger is usually disappointment.

2. Learn The History Of Family Disappointment. Often, during quarrels and heated conversations, suddenly memories of childhood abuse or disappointment in a parent reappear.

3. Learn How You Should Begin

Praying For Your Mate. One wife went into a rage when her husband was late coming home from work. She imagined infidelity. The uncontrollable rage revealed root insecurity and a sense of insignificance and unworthiness. This revelation forever changed the prayer focus of her husband. He became her faithful Intercessor.

Two Are Always Better Than One.

～ 9 ～

ESTABLISH A SPECIFIC MORNING ROUTINE FOR YOUR FAMILY ALTAR.

Reaching Proves Humility.
*Prayer is reaching...*for Divine assistance. Nothing impresses the heart of The Father more. Prayer involves God in your marriage. "And ye shall seek Me, and find Me, when ye shall search for Me with all your heart. And I will be found of you, saith the Lord:" (Jeremiah 29:13,14).

1. Embrace Prayer As The Divine Instrument For Healing. "...I have heard thy prayer, I have seen thy tears: behold, I will heal thee:" (2 Kings 20:5)

2. Establish A Specific Time To Pray Together Each Morning. Keep it brief. Though uncomfortable at first, the awkwardness dissolves when ritualized...as a part of your morning routine.

3. Set Aside A Specific Place Or Room For This Divine Appointment Each Morning With The Holy Spirit. I have sanctified my special room as...The Secret Place. Name your place whatever inspires you...The Upper Room...The War Room...My Garden of Prayer...or whatever.

4. Create A Basic Plan And Pattern For Prayer. Keep a Pictorial Prayer Book. List the names, needs and pictures for your focus. Keep a list of scriptures for Confession and Faith-building.

The Secret Of Your Success Is Always Hidden In Your Daily Routine.

RECOMMENDED BOOKS AND TAPES:
B-69   Wisdom Keys For A Powerful Prayer Life (32 pages/$3)
B-115   Seeds Of Wisdom On The Secret Place (32 pages/$5)
CD-08   Songs From The Secret Place (music CD/$30)

⁓ 10 ⁓

Exercise Your Spiritual Authority During Any Demonic Attack.

You Have An Adversary.

1. Remember Everything Good Is Despised By Everything Evil. The book of Job documents this when satan complained to God about the loyalty of Job.

2. Identify The Person Or Method Satan Uses To Introduce Anger, Agitation Or Contention. Is it a television show that stirs up jealousy, envy or fear? Is there a relationship that feeds conflict and unrest in your marriage? Pinpoint it honestly...then address it in the privacy of your prayer life.

3. Accept The Holy Spirit As The Power Source That Honors Your Position Of Authority Over Evil Influences. Any Uncontested Enemy Will Flourish. "Ye are of God, little children, and have overcome them: because greater is He that is in you, than he that is in the world" (1 John 4:4).

4. Dominate Your Home Environment

Daily With Power Praying. Walk through your home singing, worshipping and confessing the Word of God aloud. "Speaking to yourselves in psalms and hymns and spiritual songs, singing...to the Lord;" (Ephesians 5:19).

"Holy Spirit, You are welcome in this home. Nothing will be permitted that offends You. We bind and remove every evil spirit from this home. In the Name of Jesus. Amen."

❦ 11 ❦

STAY DISCREET ABOUT PROBLEMS YOU ARE EXPERIENCING IN YOUR MARRIAGE.

Talk Magnifies Everything.
When you talk about your problems to everyone, you perpetuate the memory of them. It positions you as a victim...and delays any efforts for recovery.

1. Bad News Is Remembered Longer Than Good News. So, years after you have resolved a conflict, others will continue to focus on it.

2. The Wise Never Discuss Their Problems With Someone Incapable Of Solving Them. Your chosen confidante should be competent and discreet...with a proven history of competent counsel.

3. Someone You Are Trusting Is Trusting Someone Else You Would Not. Who have your friends chosen to trust? Whose advice and companionship do they pursue?

4. Problem-Talk Portrays You As The Victim, Not The Overcomer. Nobody backs losers. When Job lost everything, everyone avoided him. It was only when God doubled his blessings that others returned to participate in his life by giving him gifts. Harness your mouth, thoughts and focus.

Silence Can Never Be Misquoted.

12

INVEST TIME IN DISCOVERING THE GOALS, DREAMS, GIFTS AND POTENTIAL OF YOUR MATE.

Diamonds Are Deep In The Earth.
Gold requires unending search and scrutiny.

1. Your Mate Is The Gold Mine Divinely Bestowed To You. God gave you what you *needed*...not what you necessarily *earned*. You were attracted to the obvious and apparent. Their greatest legacy to you is hidden, invisible and will require serious and patient pursuit.

2. You Have No Right To Anything You Have Not Pursued. That's why Jesus had the meal in the home of Zacchaeus, the evil tax collector. Zacchaeus pursued Jesus. The blind man cried out. His healing became his Harvest.

3. The Quality Of Your Questions Reveal The Depth Of Your Caring. The Scriptures documented the long journey of the Queen of Sheba. She invested nine months of travel to meet the most famous and wealthiest king in the known world...Solomon. Her questions unlocked the profound Wisdom within him and the golden relationship for their lifetime.

4. Keep A Dream-Journal. Observe. Listen. Assist. Document the desires, needs, fears and goals of your mate. *Celebrate The Dream... hidden deep in the imagination of your mate.* Protect The Dream and help them grow it.

Keeping A Dream-Journal Is Invaluable.

RECOMMENDED BOOKS:
B-127   Seeds Of Wisdom On Goal-Setting (32 pages/$5)

❧ 13 ❧

KEEP A LOVE-JOURNAL.

Memory Is A Gift Or A Curse.

You alone decide the product of your memory.

Your mind has two dominant functions: The *Imagination* and The *Memory*.

Your Imagination mentally pre-plays a *future* event.

Your Memory mentally re-plays a *past* event.

Painful moments will come. Waves of sadness will overwhelm every home, every marriage, every heart. Disappointment is inevitable. So, you must decide the joys and laughter that characterize the life you admire and desire.

1. Decide The Life Events You Want To Remember. Some are basic such as Birthdays, Anniversaries, Thanksgiving, Christmas or New Year's. Surprise moments...humorous situations...or memorable vacations require *your* planning, decision-making or *readiness*.

2. Collect Pictures Of The Events And Places You Want To Experience Together. Peruse magazines and newspapers. Question friends for their recommendations of unforgettable places or experiences.

3. Use Pictures To Record Memorable And Loving Moments. Keep a throw-away camera in your glove compartment...briefcase...in the kitchen...or wherever.

4. Seize Any Moment Worth Celebrating...And Magnify It. Others will remember wrong moments, so you must *aggressively* capture the scenes and seconds that become your Well of Memory.

5. Dignify, Memorialize And Memorize Your Journey Through Life By Keeping A Personal Love-Journal.

Any Life Worth Living Is Worth Documenting.

≈ 14 ≈

DO MONEY-TALKS TOGETHER ROUTINELY.

━━━━━━━▷•◦•◁━━━━━━━

Decisions Decide Your Wealth.

Money is a *Tool*...that builds the environment, home and circumstances you dream about.

Money is a *Communicator*...that enables you to give gifts, Pictures of Remembrance. *Gifts can talk* your love when you feel incapable of choosing the appropriate words.

1. Embrace The Financial Philosophy And Beliefs Established By The Holy Spirit In The Word Of God. The Scriptures teach that prosperity is the will of God...that Diligence, Integrity, Obedience, Parental Respect, Productivity, Tithing and Wisdom are the Seven Master Foundation Stones of Financial Wealth (see Psalm 112:1-3). Wisdom matters.

2. Set Specific Money Goals With Deadlines And Details. Choose which wall in your home will become your Dream-Wall. Keep pictures of the house, car and future you are focusing your faith toward right now. The Power is in your *Plan.*

3. Choose A Financial Mentorship Program That You Both Respect And Value. Friends or your financial advisor may recommend one for you. Select one book a month to read, underline and discuss...together.

4. Set Aside Two Hours Weekly To Review All Financial Matters Honestly And Completely. Integrity matters. Pray over your goals, plans and opportunities to solve problems for others.

Information Always Breeds Confidence.

RECOMMENDED BOOKS:

B-82   31 Reasons People Do Not Receive Their Financial Harvest (229 pages/$12)

❦ 15 ❦

DEFINE CLEARLY YOUR EXPECTATIONS OF EACH OTHER.

The Enemy Of Peace Is Confusion.

Nations, families and people fragment because of wrong words, unclear motives or undefined goals.

1. Establish A General List Of The Tasks Necessary For A Peaceful Home. This includes daily, weekly, monthly and even annual tasks. Decide clearly who is assigned to each task. Systematize the method for accountability, whether it be purchasing or paying bills.

2. Create An Environment For Mentorship And Learning. A parent once told me, "I love my child so much I even make their bed for them." I explained that she was *stealing* from her child...the golden opportunity to learning order and how to give back to a parent.

3. Recognize That Your Greatest Gift To Another Is An Opportunity To Become A Giver Instead Of A Taker. Taking comes easy. It seems to be human nature. Think of the newborn baby reaching for the milk desired...without attending any seminar on it! Those who continually receive must be given The Master Gift...*the opportunity to become* a Giver.

4. Document Your Agreement And Update It Routinely. Needs change. Focus for excellence. *Increased Information Will Always Necessitate Change.*

Bitterness Is The Product Of Unexplained Behavior.

❧ 16 ❧

NEVER ACCEPT REPORTS OF OTHERS BEFORE YOUR MATE'S EXPLANATION.

Accurate Information Matters.

Someone related that they had seen a "woman leave the hotel room" of a well-known minister. It launched a flood of accusatory statements, until someone quietly revealed...it was his sister. Incidentally, her husband had remained with the minister while she searched for the ice machine. Nobody had even considered that!

1.   Nothing Is Ever As It First Appears. Half-truth is The Backbone of Modern Media. Yet, it has destroyed the lives and families of millions. "He that answereth a matter before he heareth it, it is folly and shame unto him" (Proverbs 18:13).

2.   The First Weapon Of All Satanic Strategy Is Doubt And Unbelief. Think about the Garden of Eden. Adam and Eve were enjoying walks with God. Suddenly, the serpent injects poisonous doubt. "...Yea, hath God said, Ye shall not eat of every tree of the garden?" (Genesis 3:1). It destroyed their life and the future of the entire human race.

3. The Wise Always Mark Any Satanic Relationship That Increases Your Confusion Instead Of Your Peace. Paul said, "Be not deceived: evil communications corrupt good manners" (1 Corinthians 15:33). *Remember This.*

Missing Information Makes Conclusions Impossible.

❧ 17 ❧

PRAY FOR SPECIFIC METHODS TO MEET THE NEEDS OF YOUR MATE.

The Holy Spirit Is Your Mentor.

He knows your mate better than you. He has knowledge of the childhood pain, disappointments and fears. He knows the deepest yearnings of their heart. The Holy Spirit knows your mate more than they know themselves.

Listen to Him. Reach for His knowledge.

1. The Holy Spirit Loves Your Mate Even More Than You Ever Will. Remember this! The Spirit decided your Assignment...to them. So, He will advise, counsel and continuously mentor you on how to minister, protect and strengthen them. "I will instruct thee and teach thee in the way which thou shalt go: I will guide thee with Mine eye" (Psalm 32:8).

2. Any Sincere Prayer For Divine Wisdom Is Guaranteed An Answer From God. "If any of you lack wisdom, let him ask of God, that giveth to all men liberally, and upbraideth not; and it shall be given him" (James 1:5). The more specific your prayer request, the greater your faith.

3. What God Has Stored In You For Your Mate Is Your Point Of Difference From All Others. Expect The Holy Spirit to reveal hidden opportunities to minister *strategically.*

Small Hinges Can Swing Huge Doors.

The Secret Of Your Future
Is Hidden
In Your Daily Routine.

-MIKE MURDOCK

∞ **18** ∞

PLAY AS HARD AS YOU WORK.

═══►►-◦-◄◄═══

Rest Is As Important As Work.

Work is mentioned in the Bible 420 times. *Rest* is mentioned 275 times. Both are essential.

1.   The Season Of Rest And Renewal Is Sacred, Holy And Commanded. After creating the universe, the animals and the human race, God rested. "And God blessed the seventh day, and sanctified it: because that in it He had rested from all His work" (Genesis 2:3; see also Matthew 11:28,29).

2.   Jesus Scheduled Seasons Of Rest, Change And Renewal For His Own Disciples. "And He said unto them, Come ye yourselves apart into a desert place, and rest a while: for there were many coming and going, and they had no leisure so much as to eat" (Mark 6:31).

3.   Every Vacation Should Have A Chosen Theme. One leader chooses a different focus each year...golf, learning Spanish, or deep-sea diving. "To every thing there is a season, and a time to every purpose under the heaven" (Ecclesiastes 3:1).

4.   The Rhythm And Regularity Of Your Stress-free Fun Season Will Actually Increase

Your Productivity. "A time to weep, and a time to laugh; a time to mourn, and a time to dance" (Ecclesiastes 3:4). One pastor said, "My Friday Focus is my family exclusively. It has revolutionized our love for each other and the ministry as well. I enjoy my church now more than ever."

Any Great Habit Can Be Learned.

RECOMMENDED BOOKS:
TS-41   The School Of Wisdom, Volume 1: The Uncommon Life
        (6 tapes/$30)

19

Never Betray A Shared Confidence From Your Mate With Another.

Character Can Be Trusted.

1. Every Human Heart Contains Secrets. Every marriage mate has habits, weaknesses, fantasies, childhood memories...hidden deep inside. Unspoken needs and longings lie deep inside us. The yearning of the human heart for someone to trust is profound and unchanging.

2. God Designed Marriage To Be A Safe Haven In A Dangerous World. When God links you with the mate of His choice, you will not have to live guarded, afraid and constantly in fear.

3. Those Who Want To Be Feared... Should Be Feared. They are deadly. Those who rule through threat instead of mentorship are a satanic tool.

4. The Trustworthy Mate Is Never Dangerous. Their conduct is decided by their character, not opportunity. The Proverbs 31 Woman is thus described, "The heart of her husband doth safely trust in her," (Proverbs 31:11).

Your mate is human. Failure is inevitable. Give them what you yourself long for...the *safety of discretion.*

It is so easy to serve someone who can be trusted.

5. The Proof Of Loyalty Is Discretion. Can you be trusted with the hidden secrets confided to you by your mate?

The Marriage Without Fear Is Heaven On Earth.

❧ 20 ❧

MAKE THE WORD OF GOD THE STANDARD FOR YOUR PERSONAL CONDUCT.

The Bible Is The Master Standard.

The Word of God contains the Secrets for Successful Relationships...especially the happy marriage.

1. The Word Of God Establishes The Responsibility And Protocol Of The Husband. "Husbands, love your wives, even as Christ also loved the church, and gave Himself for it;" (Ephesians 5:25).

2. The Word Of God Establishes The Responsibility Of The Wife. "Wives, submit yourselves unto your own husbands, as unto the Lord. Therefore as the church is subject unto Christ, so let the wives be to their own husbands in every thing" (Ephesians 5:22,24).

3. The Word Of God Teaches The Desired Environment And Protocol Of The Happy Marriage Partner. "...teach the young women to be sober, to love their husbands, to love their children, To be discreet, chaste, keepers at home, good, obedient to their own husbands," (Titus 2:4,5).

4.   The Dominant Quality Of The Spirit Is Kindness...In Every Situation.

Kindness is *commanded.* "...kind one to another" (Ephesians 4:32).

The Proof of Love is *kindness.* "...[love] is kind;" (1 Corinthians 13:4).

A God-Quality. "God:...is of great kindness," (Joel 2:13).

A work of The Holy Spirit. "...kindness, by the Holy Ghost" (2 Corinthians 6:6).

Our Prayer Together...

"Father, marriage was intended to be a haven of protection, education and significance. I ask You today for the Divine Wisdom necessary to start the journey to wholeness, peace and a stress-free environment. Make me the instrument of change in Your hand. My faith is in Your power, Your promises and unchanging commitment to my home. In Jesus' name. Amen."

DECISION

Will You Accept Jesus As Your Personal Savior Today?

The Bible says, "That if thou shalt confess with thy mouth the Lord Jesus, and shalt believe in thine heart that God hath raised Him from the dead, thou shalt be saved" (Romans 10:9).

Pray this prayer from your heart today!

"Dear Jesus, I believe that You died for me and rose again on the third day. I confess I am a sinner...I need Your love and forgiveness...Come into my heart. Forgive my sins. I receive Your eternal life. Confirm Your love by giving me peace, joy and supernatural love for others. Amen."

DR. MIKE MURDOCK

is in tremendous demand as one of the most dynamic speakers in America today.

More than 14,000 audiences in 38 countries have attended his meetings and seminars. Hundreds of invitations come to him from churches, colleges and business corporations. He is a noted author of over 140 books, including the best sellers, *"The Leadership Secrets of Jesus"* and *"Secrets of the Richest Man Who Ever Lived."* Thousands view his weekly television program, *"Wisdom Keys with Mike Murdock."* Many attend his Schools of Wisdom that he hosts in major cities of America.

Clip and Mail

☐ Yes, Mike! I made a decision to accept Christ as my personal Savior today. Please send me my free gift of your book, *"31 Keys to a New Beginning"* to help me with my new life in Christ. *(B-48)*

NAME _____ BIRTHDAY _____

ADDRESS _____

CITY _____ STATE _____ ZIP _____

PHONE _____ E-MAIL _____

Mail form to:

The Wisdom Center · *P. O. Box 99* · *Denton, TX 76202*
1-888-WISDOM-1 (1-888-947-3661) · *Website:* ***thewisdomcenter.tv***

DR. MIKE MURDOCK

1 Has embraced his Assignment to Pursue...Proclaim...and Publish the Wisdom of God to help people achieve their dreams and goals.

2 Began full-time evangelism at the age of 19, which has continued since 1966.

3 Has traveled and spoken to more than 14,000 audiences in 38 countries, including East and West Africa, the Orient and Europe.

4 Noted author of 140 books, including best sellers, "Wisdom For Winning," "Dream Seeds" and "The Double Diamond Principle."

5 Created the popular "Topical Bible" series for Businessmen, Mothers, Fathers, Teenagers; "The One-Minute Pocket Bible" series, and "The Uncommon Life" series.

6 Has composed more than 5,700 songs such as "I Am Blessed," "You Can Make It," "God Rides On Wings Of Love" and "Jesus, Just The Mention Of Your Name," recorded by many gospel artists.

7 Is the Founder of The Wisdom Center, in Denton, Texas.

8 Has a weekly television program called "Wisdom Keys With Mike Murdock."

9 Has appeared often on TBN, CBN, BET and other television network programs.

10 Is a Founding Trustee on the Board of International Charismatic Bible Ministries with Oral Roberts.

11 Has had more than 3,500 accept the call into full-time ministry under his ministry.

THE MINISTRY

1 **Wisdom Books & Literature** - Over 140 best-selling Wisdom Books and 70 Teaching Tape Series.

2 **Church Crusades** - Multitudes are ministered to in crusades and seminars throughout America in "The Uncommon Wisdom Conferences." Known as a man who loves pastors he has focused on church crusades for 36 years.

3 **Music Ministry** - Millions have been blessed by the anointed songwriting and singing of Mike Murdock, who has made over 15 music albums and CDs available.

4 **Television** - "Wisdom Keys With Mike Murdock," a nationally-syndicated weekly television program.

5 **The Wisdom Center** - The Ministry Offices of The Mike Murdock Evangelistic Association where Schools of Wisdom have been held.

6 **Schools of the Holy Spirit** - Mike Murdock hosts Schools of the Holy Spirit in many churches to mentor believers on the Person and Companionship of the Holy Spirit.

7 **Schools of Wisdom** - In many major cities Mike Murdock hosts Schools of Wisdom for those who want personalized and advanced training for achieving "The Uncommon Life."

8 **Missions Outreach** - Dr Mike. Murdock's overseas outreaches to 38 countries have included crusades in East and West Africa, South America, the Orient and Europe.

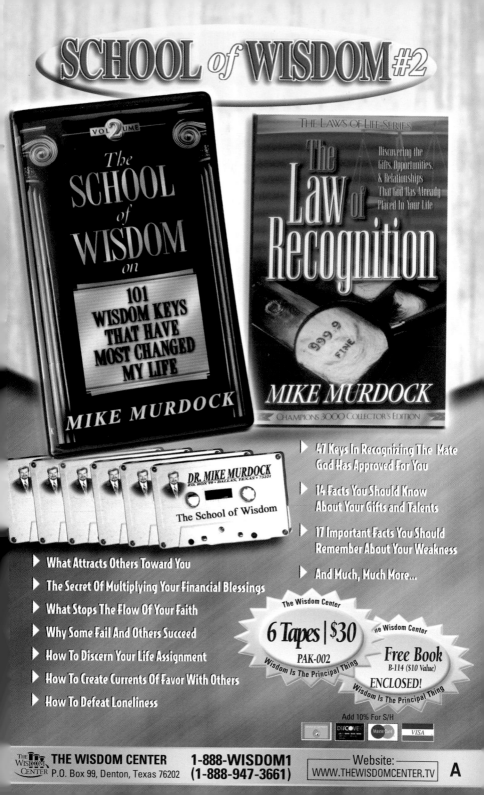

UNCOMMON WISDOM FOR UNCOMMON POWER

THE Power 7

VOLUME 13
SEEDS of WISDOM on the SECRET PLACE

VOLUME 14
SEEDS of WISDOM on the HOLY SPIRIT

VOLUME 20
SEEDS of WISDOM on YOUR ASSIGNMENT

VOLUME 23
SEEDS of WISDOM on GOAL SETTING

MY PERSONAL DREAM BOOK

101 WISDOM KEYS

31 Keys To A New Beginning

The Power 7 Pak

▶ Seeds of Wisdom on The Secret Place (B-115 / $5)
▶ Seeds of Wisdom on The Holy Spirit (B-116 / $5)
▶ Seeds of Wisdom on Your Assignment (B-122 / $5)
▶ Seeds of Wisdom on Goal Setting (B-127 / $5)
▶ My Personal Dream Book (B-143 / $5)
▶ 101 Wisdom Keys (B-45 / $5)
▶ 31 Keys To A New Beginning (B-48 / $5)

The Wisdom Center
All 7 Books Only $20
WBL-19
Wisdom Is The Principal Thing

Add 10% For S/H

THE WISDOM CENTER
P.O. Box 99, Denton, Texas 76202
1-888-WISDOM1
(1-888-947-3661)
Website:
WWW.THEWISDOMCENTER.TV

Financial Success.

VIDEO
31 REAON
PEOPLE DO NOT RECEIVE THEIR
FINANCIAL HARVE$T

MIKE MURDOCK

VIDEO
7 KEYS to 1000 TIMES MORE

The Lord God Of Your Fathers Make You A Thousand Times So Many More As You Are, And Bless You, As He Hath Promised You!
Deuteronomy 1:11

MIKE MURDOCK

▶ 8 Scriptural Reasons You Should Pursue Financial Prosperity

▶ The Secret Prayer Key You Need When Making A Financial Request To God

▶ The Weapon Of Expectation And The 5 Miracles It Unlocks

▶ How To Discern Those Who Qualify To Receive Your Financial Assistance

▶ How To Predict The Miracle Moment God Will Schedule Your Financial Breakthrough

▶ Habits Of Uncommon Achievers

▶ The Greatest Success Law I Ever Discovered

▶ How To Discern Your Place Of Assignment, The Only Place Financial Provision Is Guaranteed

▶ 3 Secret Keys In Solving Problems For Others

Songs From The Secret Place!

The Music Ministry of MIKE MURDOCK

Love Songs To The Holy Spirit Birthed In The Secret Place

THE HOLY SPIRIT HANDBOOK
What You Need To Know About Your Daily Companion, The Holy Spirit
Volume 1
MIKE MURDOCK

The Wisdom Center
6 Tapes | $30
PAK-007
Wisdom Is The Principal Thing

Free Book
B-100 ($10 Value)
ENCLOSED!
Wisdom Is The Principal Thing

Songs...

1. A Holy Place
2. Anything You Want
3. Everything Comes From You
4. Fill This Place With Your Presence
5. First Thing Every Morning
6. Holy Spirit, I Want To Hear You
7. Holy Spirit, Move Again
8. Holy Spirit, You Are Enough
9. I Don't Know What I Would Do Without You
10. I Let Go (Of Anything That Stops Me)
11. I'll Just Fall On You
12. I Love You, Holy Spirit
13. I'm Building My Life Around You
14. I'm Giving Myself To You
15. I'm In Love! I'm In Love!
16. I Need Water (Holy Spirit, You're My Well)
17. In The Secret Place
18. In Your Presence, I'm Always Changed
19. In Your Presence (Miracles Are Born)
20. I've Got To Live In Your Presence
21. I Want To Hear Your Voice
22. I Will Do Things Your Way
23. Just One Day At A Time
24. Meet Me In The Secret Place
25. More Than Ever Before
26. Nobody Else Does What You Do
27. No No Walls!
28. Nothing Else Matters Anymore (Since I've Been In The Presence Of You Lord)
29. Nowhere Else
30. Once Again You've Answered
31. Only A Fool Would Try (To Live Without You)
32. Take Me Now
33. Teach Me How To Please You
34. There's No Place I'd Rather Be
35. Thy Word Is All That Matters
36. When I Get In Your Presence
37. You're The Best Thing (That's Ever Happened To Me)
38. You Are Wonderful
39. You've Done It Once
40. You Keep Changing Me
41. You Satisfy

Add 10% For S/H

THE WISDOM CENTER
P.O. Box 99, Denton, Texas 76202
1-888-WISDOM1
(1-888-947-3661)
Website:
WWW.THEWISDOMCENTER.TV

D

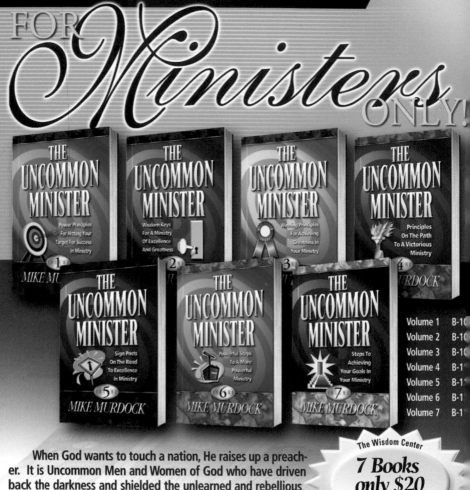

UNCOMMON WISDOM FOR AN UNCOMMON MINISTRY

FOR *Ministers* ONLY!

THE UNCOMMON MINISTER — Power Principles For Hitting Your Target For Success In Ministry — 1 — MIKE MURDOCK

THE UNCOMMON MINISTER — Wisdom Keys For A Ministry Of Excellence And Greatness — 2

THE UNCOMMON MINISTER — Winning Principles For Achieving Greatness In Your Ministry — 3

THE UNCOMMON MINISTER — Principles On The Path To A Victorious Ministry — 4

THE UNCOMMON MINISTER — Sign Posts On The Road To Excellence In Ministry — 5 — MIKE MURDOCK

THE UNCOMMON MINISTER — Powerful Steps To A More Powerful Ministry — 6 — MIKE MURDOCK

THE UNCOMMON MINISTER — Steps To Achieving Your Goals In Your Ministry — 7 — MIKE MURDOCK

Volume 1	B-1(
Volume 2	B-1(
Volume 3	B-1(
Volume 4	B-1
Volume 5	B-1
Volume 6	B-1
Volume 7	B-1

When God wants to touch a nation, He raises up a preacher. It is Uncommon Men and Women of God who have driven back the darkness and shielded the unlearned and rebellious from devastation by satanic forces. They offer the breath of life to a dead world. They open Golden Doors to Change. They unleash Forces of Truth in an age of deception.

An Uncommon Minister is prepared through seasons of pain, encounters with God, and mentors. Having sat at the feet of Uncommon Mentors his entire life, Dr. Mike Murdock shares practical but personal keys to increase the excellence and productivity of your ministry. Each volume of "The Uncommon Minister" is handy, convenient and easy to read. Your load will be lighter, your journey happier, and your effectiveness increased in "doing the will of the Father."

Add 10% For S/H

THE WISDOM CENTER BOOK DISPLAY CONTAINS 445 BOOKS!

Slot #	Item #	Title Of Books	Quantity	Retail Cost Per Book	Total Retail Value
1	B-01	Wisdom For Winning	5	$10.00 ea	$50.00
2	B-01	Wisdom For Winning	5	$10.00 ea	$50.00
3	B-11	Dream Seeds	12	$9.00 ea	$108.00
4	B-26	The God Book	7	$10.00 ea	$70.00
5	B-27	The Jesus Book	7	$10.00 ea	$70.00
6	B-28	The Blessing Bible	6	$10.00 ea	$60.00
7	B-29	The Survival Bible	6	$10.00 ea	$60.00
8	B-40	Wisdom For Crisis Times	9	$9.00 ea	$81.00
9	B-42	One-Minute Businessman's Devotional	5	$12.00 ea	$60.00
10	B-43	One-Minute Businesswoman's Devotional	5	$12.00 ea	$60.00
11	B-44	31 Secrets For Career Success	9	$10.00 ea	$90.00
12	B-45	101 Wisdom Keys	17	$5.00 ea	$85.00
13	B-46	31 Facts About Wisdom	15	$5.00 ea	$75.00
14	B-47	Covenant Of Fifty-Eight Blessings	10	$8.00 ea	$80.00
15	B-48	31 Keys To A New Beginning	15	$5.00 ea	$75.00
16	B-49	The Proverbs 31 Woman	13	$7.00 ea	$91.00
17	B-54	31 Greatest Chapters In The Bible	5	$10.00 ea	$50.00
18	B-57	31 Secrets Of An Unforgettable Woman	8	$9.00 ea	$72.00
19	B-71	Wisdom: God's Golden Key To Success	11	$7.00 ea	$77.00
20	B-72	Double Diamond Daily Devotional	3	$15.00 ea	$45.00
21	B-74	The Assignment Vol. 1: The Dream And The Destiny	8	$10.00 ea	$80.00
22	B-75	The Assignment Vol. 2: The Anointing And The Adversity	7	$10.00 ea	$70.00
23	B-82	31 Reasons People Do Not Receive Their Financial Harvest	5	$12.00 ea	$60.00
24	B-82	31 Reasons People Do Not Receive Their Financial Harvest	5	$12.00 ea	$60.00
25	B-91	The Leadership Secrets Of Jesus	6	$10.00 ea	$60.00
26	B-91	The Leadership Secrets Of Jesus	6	$10.00 ea	$60.00
27	B-92	Secrets Of Journey Vol. 1	15	$5.00 ea	$75.00
28	B-93	Secrets Of Journey Vol. 2	15	$5.00 ea	$75.00
29	B-97	The Assignment Vol. 3: The Trials And The Triumph	7	$10.00 ea	$70.00
30	B-98	The Assignment Vol. 4: The Pain And The Passion	7	$10.00 ea	$70.00
31	B-99	Secrets Of The Richest Man Who Ever Lived	6	$10.00 ea	$60.00
32	B-99	Secrets Of The Richest Man Who Ever Lived	6	$10.00 ea	$60.00
33	B-100	Holy Spirit Handbook Vol. 1	8	$10.00 ea	$80.00
34	B-101	The 3 Most Important Things In Your Life	5	$10.00 ea	$50.00
35	B-101	The 3 Most Important Things In Your Life	5	$10.00 ea	$50.00
36	B-104	7 Keys To 1000 Times More	8	$10.00 ea	$80.00
37	B-104	7 Keys To 1000 Times More	8	$10.00 ea	$80.00
38	B-107	The Uncommon Minister Vol. 1	15	$5.00 ea	$75.00
39	B-108	The Uncommon Minister Vol. 2	15	$5.00 ea	$75.00
40	B-114	The Law Of Recognition	5	$10.00 ea	$50.00
41	B-114	The Law Of Recognition	5	$10.00 ea	$50.00
42	B-115	Seeds Of Wisdom On The Secret Place Vol.13	15	$5.00 ea	$75.00
43	B-116	Seeds Of Wisdom On The Holy Spirit Vol.14	15	$5.00 ea	$75.00
44	B-117	Seeds Of Wisdom On The Word Of God Vol.15	15	$5.00 ea	$75.00
45	B-118	Seeds Of Wisdom On Problem Solving Vol.16	15	$5.00 ea	$75.00
46	B-122	Seeds Of Wisdom On Your Assignment Vol.20	15	$5.00 ea	$75.00
47	B-127	Seeds Of Wisdom On Goal-Setting Vol.25	15	$5.00 ea	$75.00
48	B-137	Seeds Of Wisdom On Productivity Vol.27	15	$5.00 ea	$75.00

Total of 445 Books and Display ~~$3,674.00~~

$1,985.00

THE WISDOM CENTER
P.O. Box 99, Denton, Texas 76202

1-888-WISDOM1
(1-888-947-3661)

Website:
WWW.THEWISDOMCENTER.TV

I

GIFTS OF WISDOM...

SPECIALTY *Bibles*

*Each Book Sold Separately

- ► The Businessman's Topical Bible (B-33 / $10)
- ► The Children's Topical Bible (B-154 / $10)
- ► The Father's Topical Bible (B-35 / $10)
- ► The Grandparent's Topical Bible (B-34 / $10)
- ► The Minister's Topical Bible (B-32 / $10)
- ► The Mother's Topical Bible (B-36 / $10)
- ► The New Believer's Topical Bible (B-37 / $10)
- ► The Seeds of Wisdom Topical Bible (B-31 / $10)
- ► The ServiceMan's Topical Bible (B-138 / $10)

- ► The Teen's Topical Bible (B-30 / $10)
- ► The Traveler's Topical Bible (B-139 / $10)
- ► The Widow's Topical Bible (B-38 / $10)

The Wisdom Center

Only $10 each

Wisdom Is The Principal Thing

Add 10% For S/H

My Gift Of Appreciation...
The Wisdom Commentary

The Wisdom Commentary includes 52 topics...for mentoring your family every week of the year.

These topics include:

- Abilities
- Achievement
- Anointing
- Assignment
- Bitterness
- Blessing
- Career
- Change
- Children
- Dating
- Depression
- Discipline
- Divorce
- Dreams And Goals
- Enemy
- Enthusiasm
- Favor
- Finances
- Fools
- Giving
- Goal-Setting
- God
- Happiness
- Holy Spirit
- Ideas
- Intercession
- Jobs
- Loneliness
- Love
- Mentorship
- Ministers
- Miracles
- Mistakes
- Money
- Negotiation
- Prayer
- Problem-Solving
- Protégés
- Satan
- Secret Place
- Seed-Faith
- Self-Confidence
- Struggle
- Success
- Time-Management
- Understanding
- Victory
- Weaknesses
- Wisdom
- Word Of God
- Words
- Work

THE Mike Murdock COLLECTOR'S EDITION

The Wisdom Commentary of MIKE MURDOCK

THE WISDOM COMMENTARY 1

B-136

Gift Of Appreciation
For Your Sponsorship Seed of $100 or More
Gift Of Appreciation

My Gift Of Appreciation To My Sponsors! ...Those Who Sponsor One Square Foot In The Completion Of The Wisdom Center!

Thank you so much for becoming a part of this wonderful project...The completion of The Wisdom Center! The total purchase and renovation cost of this facility (10,000 square feet) is just over $1,000,000. This is approximately $100 per square foot. **The Wisdom Commentary is my Gift of Appreciation for your Sponsorship Seed of $100...that sponsors one square foot of The Wisdom Center! Become a Sponsor!** You will love this Volume 1, of The Wisdom Commentary. It is my exclusive Gift of Appreciation for The Wisdom Key Family who partners with me in the Work of God as a Sponsor.

Add 10% For S/H